COLQUHOUN

SI · JE · PUIS ·

Ancient Colquhoun

Modern Colquhoun

3

CLAN
COLQUHOUN

COMPILED BY
Alan McNie

CASCADE PUBLISHING COMPANY
Jedburgh, Scotland

MADE IN SCOTLAND
100% PURE NEW WOOL
COLQUHOUN
By RODLINOCH
Scarf

4

ISBN 0 907614 36 1

Page 1 Explanation:
The illustrated tartan is the Ancient Colquhoun. The
water colour rendering is of Rossdhu, seat of Colquhoun
chiefs. The motto on the clan badge means 'If I can'. Also
depicted is the registered clan plant badge, Hazel.

5

Colquhoun *by McIan*

Rossdhu, *1793*

CLAN
COLQUHOUN

Condensed from Keltie's Scottish Highlands (1879)

The territory of the Colquhouns is in Dumbartonshire, and the principal families of the name are Colquhoun of Colquhoun and Luss, the chief of the clan, a baronet of Scotland and Nova Scotia, created in 1704, and of Great Britain in 1786; Colquhoun of Killermont and Garscadden; Colquhoun of Ardenconnel; and Colquhoun of Glenmillan. There was likewise Colquhoun of Tilliquhoun, a baronet of Scotland and Nova Scotia (1625), but this family is extinct.

The origin of the name is territorial. One tradition deduces the descent of the first possessor from a younger son of the old Earls of Lennox, because of the similarity of their armorial bearings. It is certain that they were anciently vassals of that potent house.

The immediate ancestor of the family of Luss was Humphry de Kilpatrick, who, in the reign of Alexander II, not later than 1246, obtained from Malcolm, Earl of Lennox, a grant of the lands and barony of Colquhoun, in the parish of Old or West Kilpatrick, *pro servitio unius militis, etc.,* and in consequence assumed the name of Colquhoun, instead of his own.

His grandson, Ingelram, third Colquhoun, lived in the reign of Alexander III.

His son, Humphry de Colquhoun, is witness in a charter of Malcolm, fifth Earl of Lennox, in favour of Sir John de Luss, between the years 1292-1333. The following remarkable reference to the construction of a house *ad opus Culquhanorum,* by order of King Robert Bruce, is extracted from the *Compotum Constabularii de Cardross,* vol. i., in the accounts of the Great Chamberlains of Scotland under date 30th July 1329, as quoted by Mr Tytler in the appendix to the second volume of his History of Scotland: "Item, in construccione cujusdam domus ad opus *Culquhanorum* Domini Regis ibidem, 10 solidi." Mr Tytler in a Regis ibidem, 10 solidi." Mr Tytler in a note says that *Culquhanorum* is "an obscure word, which occurs nowhere else – conjectured by a learned friend to be 'keepers of the dogs', from the Gaelic root *Gillen-au-con* — abbreviated, *Gillecon,* Colquhoun."

Sir Robert de Colquhoun, supposed by Mr Fraser, the family historian, to be fifth in descent from the first Humphry, and son of a Humphy, the fourth of Colquhoun, in the reign of David Bruce, married in or previous to the year 1368 the daughter and sole heiress (known in the family tradition as "The Fair Maid of Luss"), of Godfry de Luss, lord of Luss, head or chief of an ancient family of that name, and the sixth in a direct male line from Maldluin, dean of Lennox, who, in the beginning of the thirteenth century, received from Alwyn, second Earl of Lennox, a charter of the lands of Luss. The Luss territories lie in the mountainous but beautiful and picturesque district on the margin of Loch Lomond. Sir Robert was designed "dominus de Colquhoun and de Luss," in a charter dated in 1368; since which time the family have borne the designation of Colquhoun of Colquhoun and Luss. He is also witness in a charter of the lands of Auchmar by Walter of Faslane, Lord of Lennox, to Walter de Buchanan in 1373. He had four sons, namely – Sir Humphry, his heir; Robert, first of the family of Camstraddan, from whom several other families of the name of Colquhoun in Dumbartonshire are descended; Robert mentioned in the Camstraddan charter as "frater junior"; and Patrick, who is mentioned in a charter from his brother Sir Humphry to his other brother Robert.

The eldest son, Sir Humphry, sixth of Colquhoun, and eighth of Luss, is a witness in three charters by Duncan, Earl of Lennox, in the years 1393, 1394 and 1395. He died in 1406, and left three sons and two daughters. Patrick, his youngest son, was ancestor of the

Great Seal of
Robert the Bruce

Colquhouns of Glennis, from whom the Colquhouns of Barrowfield, Piemont, and others were descended. The second son, John, succeeded his eldest brother. The eldest son, Sir Robert, died in 1408, and was succeeded by his brother. Sir John Colquhoun was appointed governor of the castle of Dumbarton, by King James I, for his fidelity to that king during his imprisonment in England. From his activity in punishing the depredations of the Highlanders, who often committed great outrages in the low country of Dumbartonshire, he rendered himself obnoxious to them, and a plot was formed for his destruction. He received a civil message from some of their chiefs, desiring a friendly conference, in order to accommodate all their differences. Suspecting no treachery, he went out to meet them but slightly attended, and was immediately attacked by a numerous body of Islanders, under two noted robber-chiefs, Lachlan Maclean and Murdoch Gibson, and slain in Inchmurren, on Loch Lomond, in 1439. By his wife, Jean, daughter of Robert, Lord Erskine, he had a son, Malcolm, a youth of great promise. He died before his father, leaving a son, John, who succeeded his grandfather in 1439. This Sir John Colquhoun was one of the most distinguished men of his age in Scotland, and highly esteemed by King James III, from whom he got a charter in 1457 of the lands of Luss, Colquhoun, and Garscube, in Dumbartonshire, and of the lands of Glyn and Sauchie, in Stirlingshire, incorporating the whole into a free barony, to be called the Barony of Luss; and in the following year he obtained from the king a charter erecting into a free forest the lands of Rossdhu and Glenmachome. From 1465 to 1469 he held the high office of comptroller of the Exchequer, and was subsequently appointed sheriff principal of Dumbartonshire. In 1645 he got a grant of the lands of Kilmardinny, and in 1473 and in 1474, of Roseneath, Strone, etc. In 1474 he was appointed lord high chamberlain of Scotland, and immediately thereafter was nominated one of the ambassadors extraordinary to the Court of England, to negotiate a marriage between the Prince Royal of Scotland and the Princess Cicily, daughter of King Edward IV. By a royal charter dated 17th September 1477, he was constituted governor of the castle of Dumbarton for life. He was killed by a cannon-ball at the siege of Dumbarton Castle, probably in 1478. By his wife, daughter of Thomas, Lord Boyd, he had two sons and one daughter. His second son, Robert, was bred

Roseneath Church & Manse

Dumbarton Castle, *1874*

to the church, and was first rector of Kippen and Luss, and afterwards bishop of Argyle from 1473 to 1499. The daughter, Margaret, married Sir William Murray, seventh baron of Tullibardine (ancestor of the Dukes of Athole), and bore to him seventeen sons.

His eldest son, Sir Humphry Colquhoun, died in 1493, and was succeeded by his son, Sir John Colquhoun, who received the honour of knighthood from King James IV and obtained a charter under the great seal of sundry lands and baronies in Dumbartonshire, dated 4th December 1506. On 11th July 1526 he and Patrick Colquhoun, his son, received a respite for assisting John, Earl of Lennox, in treasonably besieging, taking, and holding the castle of Dumbarton. He died before 16th August 1536. By his first wife, Elizabeth Stewart, daughter of John, Earl of Lennox, Sir John Colquhoun had four sons and four daughters; and by his second wife, Margaret, daughter of William Cunningham of Craigends, he had two sons and two daughters. His eldest son, Sir Humphry Colquhoun, married Lady Catherine Graham, daugther of William, first Earl of Montrose, and died in 1537. By her he had three sons and two daughters. His son James, designated of Garscube, ancestor of the Colquhouns of Garscube, Adam and Patrick. His eldest son, Sir John Colquhoun, married, first, Christian Erskine, daughter of Robert, Lord Erskine; and secondly, Agnes, daughter of the fourth Lord Boyd, ancestor of the Earls of Kilmarnock. He died in 1575.

His eldest son, Humphry, acquired the heritable coronership of the county of Dumbarton, from Robert Graham of Knockdollian, which was ratified and confirmed by a charter under the great seal in 1583.

In July 1592, some of the Macgregors and Macfarlanes came down upon the low country of Dumbartonshire, and committed vast ravages, especially upon the territory of the Colquhouns. At the head of his vassals, and accompanied by several of the gentlemen of the neighbourhood, Sir Humphry Colquhoun attacked the invaders, and after a bloody conflict, which was only put an end to at nightfall, he was overpowered by his assailants, and forced to retreat. To quote from Mr Fraser's *Chiefs of the Colquhouns* –

"He betook himself to the castle of Bannachra, a stronghold which had been erected by the Colquhouns at the foot of the north side of the hill of

Bennibuie, in the parish of Luss. A party of the Macfarlanes and Macgregors pursued him, and laid siege to his castle. One of the servants who attended the knight was of the same surname as himself. He had been tampered with by the assailants of his master, and treacherously made him their victim. The servant, while conducting his master to his room up a winding stair of the castle, made him by preconcert a mark for the arrows of the clan who pursued him by throwing the glare of a paper torch upon his person when opposite a loophole. A winged arrow, darted from its string with a steady aim, pierced the unhappy knight to the heart, and he fell dead on the spot. The fatal loophole is still pointed out, but the stair, like its unfortunate lord, has crumbled into dust.''

Sir Humphry married, first, Lady Jean Cunningham, daughter of Alexander, fifth Earl of Glencairn, widow of the Earl of Argyll, by whom he had no children, and secondly, Jean, daughter of John, Lord Hamilton, by whom he had a daughter. Having no male issue, he was succeeded by his younger brother, Alexander.

In Sir Alexander's time occurred the raid of Glenfinlas, and the bloody clan conflict of Glenfruin, between the Colquhouns and Macgregors, in December 1602 and February 1603, regarding which the popular accounts are much at variance with the historical facts. The Colquhouns had taken part in the execution of the letters of fire and sword issued by the crown against the Macgregors some years before, and the feud between them had been greatly aggravated by various acts of violence and aggression on both sides.

In 1602, the Macgregors made a regular raid on the laird of Luss's lands in Glenfinlas, and carried off a number of sheep and cattle, as well as slew several of the tenants. Alexander Colquhoun, who had before complained to the privy council against the Earl of Argyll for not repressing the clan Gregor, but who had failed in obtaining any redress, now adopted a tragic method in order to excite the sympathy of the king. He appeared before his majesty at Stirling, accompanied by a number of females, the relatives of those who had been killed or wounded at Glenfinlas, each carrying the bloody shirt of her killed or wounded relative, to implore his majesty to avenge the wrongs done them. The ruse had the desired effect upon the king, who, from a sensitiveness of constitutional temperament, which made him shudder even at the sight of blood, was extremely susceptible to impressions from scenes of this description, and he immediately granted a

Stirling Castle

Loch Lomond, *looking south*

commission of lieutenancy to the laird of Luss, investing him with power to repress similar crimes, and to apprehend the perpetrators.

"This commission granted to their enemy appears to have roused the lawless rage of the Macgregors, who rose in strong force to defy the laird of Luss; and Glenfruin, with its disasters and sanguinary defeat of the Colquhouns, and its ultimate terrible consequences to the victorous clan themselves, was the result."

In the beginning of the year 1603, Allaster Macgregor of Glenstrae, followed by four hundred men chiefly of his own clan, but including also some of the clans Cameron and Anverich, armed with "halberschois, pow-aixes, twa-handir swordis, bowis and arrowis, and with hagbutis and pistoletis", advanced into the territory of Luss. Colquhoun, acting under his royal commission, had raised a force which has been stated by some writers as having amounted to 300 horse and 500 foot. This is probably an exaggeration, but even if it is not, the disasters which befell them may be explained from the trap into which they fell, and from the nature of the ground on which they encountered the enemy. This divested them of all the advantages which they might have derived from superiority of numbers and from their horse.

On the 7th February, 1603, the Macgregors were in Glenfruin "in two divisions", writes Mr Fraser — "One of them at the head of the glen, and the other in ambuscade near the farm of Strone, at a hollow or ravine called the Crate. The Colquhouns came into Glenfruin from the Luss side, which is opposite Strone — probably by Glen Luss and Glen Mackurn. Alexander Colquhoun pushed on his forces in order to get through the glen before encountering the Macgregors; but, aware of his approach, Allaster Macgregor also pushed forward one division of his forces and entered at the head of the glen in time to prevent his enemy from emerging from the upper end of the glen, whilst his brother, John McGregor, with the division of his clan, which lay in ambuscade, by a detour, took the rear of the Colquhouns, which prevented their retreat down the glen without fighting their way through that section of the Macgregors who had got in their rear. The success of the stratagem by which the Colquhouns were thus placed between two fires seems to be the only way of accounting for the terrible slaughter of the Colquhouns and the much less loss of the Macgregors.

"The Colquhouns soon became unable to maintain their ground, and, falling into a moss at the farm of Auchingaich, they were thrown into disorder, and made a hasty and disorderly retreat, which proved even more disastrous than the conflict, for they had to force their way through the men led by John Macgregor, whilst they were pressed behind by Allaster, who, reuniting the two divisions of his army, continued the pursuit."

All who fell into the hands of the victors were at once put to death, and the chief of the Colquhouns barely escaped with his life after his horse had been killed under him. One hundred and forty of the Colquhouns were slaughtered, and many more were wounded, among whom were several women and children. When the pursuit ended, the work of spoliation and devastation commenced. Large numbers of horse, cattle, sheep and goats were carried off, and many of the houses and steading of the tenantry were burned to the ground. Their triumph the Macgregors were not allowed long to enjoy. The government took instant and severe measures against them. A price was put upon the heads of seventy or eighty of them by name, and upon a number of their confederates of other clans — "Before any judicial inquiry was made", says Mr Fraser, "on 3d April 1603, only two days before James VI left Scotland for England to take possession of the English throne, an Act of Privy Council was passed, by which the name of Gregor or Macgregor was for ever abolished. All of this surname were commanded, under the penalty of death, to change it for another; and the same penalty was denounced against those who should give food or shelter to any of the clan. All who had been at the conflict at Glenfruin, and at the spoliation and burning of the lands of the Laird of Luss, were prohibited, under the penalty of death, from carrying any weapon except a pointless knife to eat their meat." Thirty-five of the clan Gregor were executed after trial between the 20th May 1603 and the 2d March 1604. Amongst these was Allaster Macgregor, who surrendered himself to the Earl of Argyll.

By his wife Helen, daughter of Sir George Buchanan of that ilk, Alexander had one son and five daughters. He died in 1617.

The eldest son, Sir John, in his father's lifetime, got a charter under the great seal of the ten pound land of Dunnerbuck, dated 20th February 1602, was created a baronet of Nova Scotia by patent dated the last day of August 1625. He married Lady Lillias Graham, daughter

Old Rossdhu Castle

of the fourth Earl of Montrose, brother of the great Marquis, by whom he had three sons and three daughters. His two eldest sons succeeded to the baronetcy. From Alexander, the third son, the Colquhouns of Tillyquhoun were descended. He died in 1647.

Sir John, the second baronet of Luss, married Margaret, daughter and sole heiress of Sir Gideon Baillie of Lochend, in the county of Haddington, and had two sons, and seven daughters. He adhered firmly to the royal cause during all the time of the civil wars, on which account he suffered many hardships, and, in 1654, was by Cromwell fined two thousand pounds sterling. He was succeeded in 1676 by his younger son, Sir James – the elder having predeceased him – third baronet of Luss, who held the estates only four years, and being a minor, unmarried, left no issue. He was succeeded in 1680 by his uncle, Sir James, who married Penuel, daughter of William Cunningham of Balleichan, in Ireland. He had, with one daughter, two sons, Sir Humphry, fifth baronet, and James. The former was a member of the last Scottish Parliament, and strenuously opposed and voted agaisnt every article of the treaty of union. By his wife Margaret, daughter of Sir Patrick Houston of that ilk, baronet, he had an only daughter, Anne Colquhoun, his sole heiress, who, in 1702, married James Grant of Pluscardine, second son of Ludovick Grant of Grant, immediate younger brother of Brigadier Alexander Grant, heir apparent of the said Ludovick.

Having no male issue, Sir Humphry, with the design that his daughter and her husband should succeed him in his whole estate and honours, in 1704 resigned his baronetcy into the hands of her majesty Queen Anne, for a new patent to himself in liferent, and his son-in-law and his heirs therein named in fee, but with this express limitation that he and his heirs so succeeding to that estate and title should be obliged to bear the name and arms of Colquhoun of Luss, etc. It was also specially provided that the estates of Grant and Luss should not be conjoined.

Sir Humphry died in 1718, and was succeeded in his estate and honours by James Grant, his son-in-law, under the name and designation of Sir James Colquhoun of Luss. He enjoyed that estate and title till the death of his elder brother, Brigadier Alexander Grant, in 1719, when, succeeding to the estate of Grant, he relinquished the

Old Parliament Buildings

name and title of Colquhoun of Luss, and resumed his own, retaining the baronetcy, it being by the last patent vested in her person. He died in 1747.

By the said Anne, his wife, he had a numerous family. His eldest son, Humphry Colquhoun, subsequently Humphry Grant of Grant, died unmarried in 1732. The second son, Ludovick, became Sir Ludovick Grant of Grant, baronet, while the fourth son James succeeded as Sir James Colquhoun of Luss, the third son having died in infancy. He is the amiable and very polite gentleman described by Smollett in his novel of Humphry Clinker, under the name of "Sir George Colquhoun, a colonel in the Dutch service." He married Lady Helen Sutherland, daughter of William Lord Strathnaver, son of the Earl of Sutherland, and by her he had three sons and five daughters. In 1777 he founded the town of Helensburgh on the firth of Clyde, and named it after his wife. To put an end to some disputes which had arisen with regard to the destination of the old patent of the Nova Scotia baronetcy, (John Colquhoun of Tillyquhoun, as the eldest cadet, having, on the death of his cousin-german, Sir Humphry Colquhoun, in 1718, assumed the title as heir male of his grandfather, the patentee), Sir James was, in 1786, created a baronet of Great Britain. His second youngest daughter, Margaret, married William Baillie, a lord of session, under the title of Lord Polkemmet, and was the mother of Sir William Baillie, baronet. Sir James died in November 1786.

His eldest son, Sir James Colquhoun, second baronet under the new patent, sheriff-depute of Dumbartonshire, was one of the principal clerks of session. By his wife, Mary, daughter and co-heir of James Falconer, Esq. of Monktown, he had seven sons and four daughters. He died in 1805. His eldest son, Sir James, third baronet, was for some time Member of Parliament for Dumbartonshire.

"Some time after Sir James' succession," says Mr Fraser, to whose book on the Colquhouns we have been much indebted in this account, "significant testimony was given that the ancient feud between his family and that of the Macgregors, which had frequently led to such disastrous results to both, had given place to feelings of hearty goodwill and friendship. On an invitation from Sir James and Lady Colquhoun, Sir John Murray Macgregor and Lady Macgregor came on a visit to Rossdhu. The two baronets visited Glenfruin. They were

Loch Lomond, looking south

Ben Lomond

accompanied by Lady Colquhoun and Misses Helen and Catherine Colquhoun. After the battlefield had been carefully inspected by the descendants of the combatants, Sir J. M. Macgregor insisted on shaking hands with Sir James Colquhoun and the whole party on the spot were it was supposed that the battle had been hottest. On the occasion of the same visit to Rossdhu, the party ascended Ben Lomond, which dominates so grandly over Loch Lomond. On the summit of this lofty mountain, Sir John M. Macgregor danced a Highland reel with Miss Catherine Colquhoun, afterwards Mrs Millar of Earnoch. Sir John was then fully eighty years of age.''

His eldest son, Sir James Colquhoun, the fourth baronet of the new creation, and the eighth of the old patent, succeeded on his father's death, 3rd February, 1836; chief of the Colquhouns of Luss; Lord-lieutenant of Dumbartonshire, and M.P. for that county from 1837 to 1841. He married in June 1843, Jane, daughter of Sir Robert Abercromby of Birkenbog. She died 3rd May 1844, leaving one son, James, born in 1844. He, as fifth baronet, succeeded his father, who was drowned in Loch Lomond, December 18, 1873.

The family mansion, Ross-dhu, is situated on a beautiful peninsula. To the possessions of the family of Colquhoun was added in 1852 the estate of Ardincaple, purchased from the Duchess Dowager of Argyll. According to Mr Fraser, the three baronets of Luss, before Sir James, purchased up no less than fourteen lairdships.

Some Associated Names

Associated names have a hazy history. Sometimes they had more than one origin; also clouding the precise location of a particular surname might be that name's proscription or of course a migrant population. Even the spelling of surnames was subject to great variations, shifting from usually Latin or Gaelic and heeding rarely to consistent spelling. In early records there can be several spellings of the same name. Undoubtedly contributing to this inconsistency is the handwriting in official records, which was often open to more than one spelling interpretation. There is no official registered list of sept names but the names listed have clan association.

With regard to the 'Mac' prefix, this was, of course, from the Gaelic meaning, son of. It wasn't long before it was abbreviated to 'Mc' or 'M', until we have reached the position now where there are more 'Mc's' than 'Mac's'.

COWAN, COWANS, COWEN, MACCOWAN The common pronunciation of Colquhoun is Cohoon. Cowan is a corruption of that name most often found in the Lowlands. The name may also derive from the Scots 'cowan' meaning a dry-stone diker. John Cowan, a merchant, founded Cowan's Hospital in Stirling in 1639. Bearing another form of MacCowan, John Mackilquhone was in Kilmarnock in 1528. John McCoan lived in Duchre, parish of Kilbrandon in 1691 (on Firth of Lorne, Argyllshire). In 1550 David M'Kowin was a notary in Glasgow. Several books belonging to the great-grandfather of Sir John Cowan of Beeslack (1m N Penicuik) bore the name Colquhoun. The English equivalent of the Gaelic MacComhan in Argyllshire is Cowan.

KILPATRICK, KIRKPATRICK The lands of Colquhoun are in the parish of Old Kilpatrick (5m SE Dumbarton). Humphrey Kilpatrick of Kirkpatrick received a grant of these lands from the Earl of Lennox in about 1241 and from then on took the name of Colquhoun from the lands. John Kylpatrick was abbot of St. Colm's Inch in 1495. (Inchcolm — 1m S of Aberdour.) In 1669 Thomas Kilpatrick recorded in East Calder (11m SW Edinburgh). Homage was rendered by John de Kirkpatrike of Dumfries-shire in 1296. A knight, Roger de Kirkpatrike of Dumfriesshire swore fealty to England in 1296. The Kirkpatrick name was derived from a chapel dedicated to St. Patrick, giving the name to a farm in the parish of Closeburn (11m NW Dumfries). Ivo Kirkpatrick and his heirs received a charter from Robert Bruce of some land between Blawatwood and the waters of Esk in 1190. Robert de Kirkpatrick was witness to confirmation of a fishery in Torduff circa 1194-1211 (5m SE Arran).

MACCLINTOCK, MACCLINTON, MACLINTOCK   The Maclintocks came from Luss and the surrounding area. In the reign of King David Bruce, 1329-1370, the lands of Luss were acquired by Sir Robert Kilpatrick of Colquhoun who married the Fair Maid of Luss. Until this marriage the lands had been held by the Earls of Lennox, an ancient family who had lived there more than 700 years. In 1549, Duncan Mcgellentak was a witness in Balquhidder (3m SW of Lochearnhead). In 1611 some Maclintocks changed their name to the more English Lindsay. John M'Inlaintaig lived in Colgine, Kilbride in 1693 (4m S of Tighnabruaich). The last of the Breadalbane smugglers was John M'Inlaintaig (W. Perthshire). Finlay Macklintoun lived in Torpichen in 1394 (2m NW Bathgate).

Loch Lomond, *looking north*

Colquhoun Country
DETAIL MAP OVERLEAF

The map used below and overleaf is intended basically as a pictorial reference. It is accurate enough, however, to be correlated with a current map. The clan boundaries are only marginally correct. No precise boundaries were kept in early times and territories were fluctuating frequently.

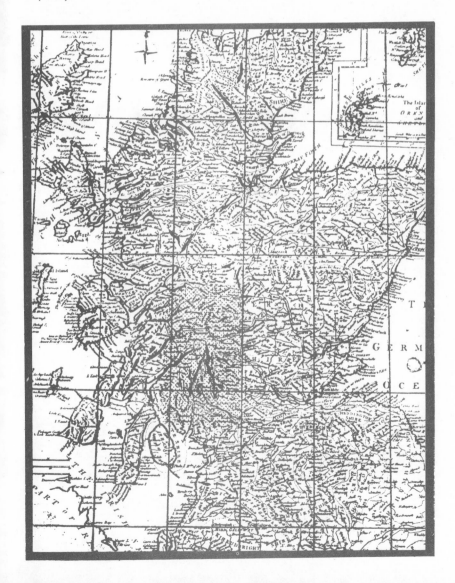

COLQUHOUN
CLAN MAP

1. Achnheaglis Ancient Colquhoun burial place

2. Bannachra, Castle of Colquhouns under MacFarlane & MacGregor siege

3. Barrowfield Cadet branch of Colquhouns here

4. Ben Lomond Impressive backdrop to view from clan country

5. Cameron Former Colquhoun holding

6. Dumbarton Castle Sir John Colquhoun of Luss served as governor

7. Dunglass Castle Ancient clan seat

8. Glenfruin Massacre Led to MacGregor proscription

9. Helensburgh Named after chief's wife, Lady Helen Sutherland, 1777

10. Inchmurrin Castle Sir John Colquhoun slain here in ambush

11. Inchlonaig Castle Sir James Colquhoun and Rob Roy met on this island

12. Kilpatrick (Old) Immediate ancestors of Luss family here

13. Luss 14th cent. acquisition by Colquhouns

14. Roseneath In 1474 was Colquhoun property

15. Rossdhu Present clan seat

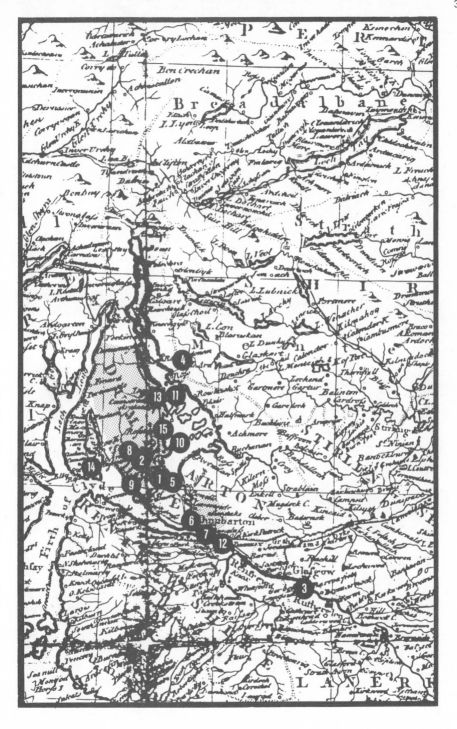

Some Clan Notables

Colquhoun, Archibald Campbell (-1820) This member of the Killermont Colquhouns was a reforming lawyer. He was one of commissioners who enquired into the administration of justice in Scotland. As well he served as member of parliament for the Elgin district of burghs.

Colquhoun, Patrick (1745-1820) From clan country this energetic and concerned citizen was commercially successful in Virginia by the age of 16. Returning to Scotland he had marked success there in business as well. His community achievements were also apparent;he became provost of Glasgow and founded the Glasgow Chamber of Commerce. On moving to London his preoccupation became the wider community: he established soup kitchens there; became a metropolitan police magistrate; wrote widely on social issues, local, national and international. His treatises were filled with practical suggestions, many of them acted on.

Colquhoun, John Campbell (1785-1854) A Colquhoun of Luss, this law and philosophy graduate at an early stage showed exceptional interest in the study of psychlical research. He wrote widely on this emerging science and its related fields, at times using the results of his own observation and research. Apart from this interest he served as sheriff-depute of Dumbarton.

Colquhoun, Daniel (1849-1935) A Glaswegian who established a distinguished medical career at Dunedin, New Zealand. He was also appointed lecturer on the practice of medicine at Otaga University. On retirement in England he was representative of the New Zealand Red Cross.

Colquhoun, Walter A. (1898-1962) This native of Wolfville, N.S., Canada was an outstanding student of pharmacy who became president of Canadian Wholesale Drugs Ltd.

Rob Roy Macgregor

Sir James Colquhoun & Rob Roy met on Inchlonaig

34

ACKNOWLEDGEMENT
We are indebted to staff members of the Scottish Room, Edinburgh City Libraries for their
generous assistance.

Research work done by Barbara Blackburn has proved valuable and thorough.